BASIC SKILLS
FOR THE
NEW MEDIATOR

Second Edition

Books by Allan H. Goodman

Basic Skills for the New Mediator

Basic Skills for the New Arbitrator

BASIC SKILLS
FOR THE
NEW MEDIATOR

Second Edition

ALLAN H. GOODMAN

SOLOMON PUBLICATIONS

Printed in the United States of America

First Printing, Second Edition   October 2004

Published and Distributed in the United States and Canada by:

Solomon Publications
PO Box 2124 Rockville, MD 20847-2124
(301) 816-1025
book@solomonpublications.com
www.solomonpublications.com

Library of Congress Catalog Number 2004093334

ISBN 0-9670973-3-9

About the Author

Allan H. Goodman is a private mediator and arbitrator. He is also a mediator and arbitrator trainer and the author of the companion volume BASIC SKILLS FOR THE NEW ARBITRATOR.

He is a graduate of the Georgetown University School of Foreign Service and the University of Toledo College of Law and is a member of the bars of District of Columbia, Maryland, and Virginia.

From 1975 to 1993 he was an attorney in private practice. He is currently a Judge on the United States Civilian Board of Contract Appeals.

Brief Table of Contents

Contents

THE JOINT SESSION -
THE MEDIATOR'S OPENING STATEMENT 52

Contents

INTRODUCTION TO THE SECOND EDITION

I wrote **Basic Skills for the New Mediator** ten years ago, after serving as a private mediator for several years. I have continued to practice as a private mediator and mediator trainer. I have added to my knowledge of the mediation process by serving in increasingly complex cases, working with fellow mediators, and hearing the experiences of those that I have trained.

The first edition of this book has been extremely well received, and I have benefited from many comments and questions from readers. The increase in the use of alternative dispute resolution techniques has sparked a tremendous interest among attorneys and other professionals to serve as mediators in their fields of expertise.

It is now time to issue a second edition to share my additional experiences and those of my colleagues and readers. Many have suggested that the book would be even more useful with a topic index, in addition to the detailed table of contents listing the 100 questions. I have therefore included an expanded index in the back of the book.

INTRODUCTION TO THE FIRST EDITION

Mediation is probably the least understood method of alternative dispute resolution. It is often confused with arbitration, and many people use the terms arbitration and mediation interchangeably.

The mediation process allows the parties to a dispute to select a neutral individual, known as the mediator, to aid them in reaching a settlement. The mediator does not decide who prevails, but facilitates discussions between the parties.

Mediation is faster and less costly than arbitration or litigation. When mediation is used effectively, even the most difficult issues can be resolved to the satisfaction of the parties, without the time, expense, and emotional toll exacted by other means of dispute resolution.

I derive a great deal of satisfaction from acting as a mediator. The mediator may communicate directly and confidentially with the parties and work with them to seek a solution. The non-adversarial nature of the process and the parties' willingness to resolve the dispute creates an environment that may lead to a settlement that is satisfactory to all.

I am amazed at the swiftness of mediation and the magnitude of the disputes that are settled. The parties are often surprised at the effectiveness of the process. The extent to which they may have compromised their claims in order to achieve settlement is justified by the savings in legal fees and other costs which would have been incurred if other methods of dispute resolution had been used.

This book suggests answers to one hundred questions new mediators have asked about the mediation process. The answers are based upon my experience as a mediator, and are solely my opinions.

Please note that Question No. 101 is your question to ask me. I also welcome other suggestions or comments.

ONE HUNDRED QUESTIONS AND ANSWERS

This book is written to be read from start to finish, and also as a reference if you are involved in a mediation session and need a quick answer. The answers to many of the questions are my opinions. You may be able to offer a more complete or creative answer. You also may think my answer is wrong. I welcome the opportunity to share your comments. Please write to me at the address provided at the end of the book.

Questions are arranged in the chronological order of the mediation process. In **THE MEDIATION PROCESS** and **THE ROLE OF THE MEDIATOR**, we discuss the general concepts of mediation and the mediator's role, including the duty of disclosure. **PRELIMINARY PROCEDURES** focuses upon the preliminary conference as a procedural means to educate the parties about the mediation process and to request information necessary before and during the mediation session.

The majority of the questions, as you would expect, are contained in the sections which discuss the mediation session. In **PHYSICAL SETTING AND GENERAL PROCEDURE**, I present an overview of the facilities that are needed to conduct a mediation, and the procedures required for effective mediation. The actual mediation session is described in detail in **THE JOINT SESSION - THE PARTIES' OPENING STATEMENTS, THE JOINT SESSION - THE MEDIATOR'S OPENING STATEMENT, THE FIRST PRIVATE CAUCUS,** and **THE SECOND PRIVATE CAUCUS AND BEYOND - ACHIEVING SETTLEMENT.**

AFTER THE MEDIATION discusses the mediator's conduct after the mediation is concluded.

Tips on arranging for compensation are included in **GETTING PAID**.

Appendix A is a sample agreement between the mediator and the parties.

Appendix B is a summary entitled "The Stages of Mediation".

Finally, **Appendix C** is a primer on the primary concepts of evidence, which I call "Everything You Never Wanted to Know About the Rules of Evidence." While it is not necessary for mediators to enforce the rules of evidence, an understanding of the issues discussed in this appendix will be useful in assessing the parties' positions in mediation. For those mediators who are not attorneys, you will probably at some point have to deal with attorneys and evidentiary vocabulary. This appendix will help you understand the basic concepts.

The Mediation
Process

THE MEDIATION PROCESS

1. What is mediation?

Mediation is a process in which a neutral individual, selected by the parties to a dispute, aids the parties in their settlement discussions and attempts to have the parties negotiate a resolution of the dispute.

2 What is the goal of mediation?

The goal of mediation is to settle the dispute. The mediator aids the parties in arriving at a settlement, but has no authority to compel a resolution of the dispute. While it is possible that the parties may not agree to a settlement, even with the help of the mediator, mediation usually does result in a settlement.

3. Why does mediation work?

In a society that thrives on courtroom drama, it often comes as a surprise that a majority of civil suits are settled before trial. Settlements result for many reasons, but often it is simply because the value of resolving a dispute may be worth more than the cost of prolonging the dispute. Many parties realize that litigation in court is expensive in more ways than one, even if they are convinced that they are right and the other party is wrong. This expense consists of legal fees, as well as the cost of the time the parties spend away from their own jobs.

When I was an attorney, I would tell my clients that when I was dealing with their lawsuits, I was at my job - when they were dealing with a lawsuit, they were away from their jobs. Lawsuits also delay the resolution of the dispute. Extensive and costly pre-trial discovery and preparation are required. Parties may wait months or years on a crowded docket before the matter comes to trial.

With today's emphasis on alternative dispute resolution, or ADR is it is commonly known, the press is giving attention to mediation as an alternative to litigation. As the public has become educated to the advantages of mediation, there has been an increased demand for the process, and for well-trained mediators.

4. How does mediation work?

The mediation process begins with the assumption that the parties are willing to settle their dispute, by compromise or other means. The parties recognize that they may not be able to resolve the dispute by dealing directly with each other. Therefore, they select a neutral third party who will help them resolve their dispute.

By exploring the strengths and weaknesses of each party's position and acting as an intermediary, the mediator provides an objective point of view and defuses the parties' emotions. The parties may reveal confidential information and settlement positions to the mediator during private, *ex parte*, caucuses. At appropriate times, the parties authorize the mediator to transmit settlement offers. A dialogue between the parties is established through the mediator. The end result is usually a settlement.

5. What is the difference between mediation and arbitration?

Arbitration is a process that is often confused with mediation. When parties to a dispute choose arbitration as a dispute resolution method, they confer upon the arbitrator the authority to hear the evidence and then render a binding decision, called an "award." The parties attempt to prove their case by presenting testimony of witnesses and relevant documentation. The arbitrator considers the evidence and decides which party will prevail. Unlike an arbitrator, the mediator does not have the authority to decide which party should prevail. The mediator acts as a facilitator of the parties' settlement discussions. Sometimes mediation results in a settlement, sometimes it does not.

6. Is mediation the same as nonbinding arbitration?

Most arbitration is **binding arbitration**, in which the parties agree in advance to abide by the decision of the arbitrator. In **nonbinding arbitration**, the parties do not agree to be bound by the arbitrator's decision. However, the process is generally the same as binding arbitration. The parties present information, in a manner similar to courtroom presentation, to an arbitrator. The arbitrator cannot have *ex parte* contact with the parties. The arbitrator then renders a nonbinding opinion, based upon the evidence presented. In nonbinding arbitration, the parties may nevertheless abide by an arbitrator's decision, if they have confidence in the arbitrator's decision and a desire to end the dispute without resorting to what probably would be lengthy and costly litigation.

Mediation is not the same as nonbinding arbitration. In nonbinding arbitration, the goal of the process is to present information to the arbitrator so that the arbitrator may render an opinion as to which party prevails. In mediation, the goal of the process is to have the parties compromise and reach a settlement. The mediator is not restricted to listening to information in the format similar to a courtroom presentation, nor does the mediator render a decision. The mediator may have, and usually does have, *ex parte* contact with the parties. Instead, the parties reach an agreement. This agreement is reduced to writing and signed by the parties. As such, it is a binding contract, and if a party fails to comply with the agreement, it can be enforced in court.

7. What if both parties have claims against each other?

The dispute may involve a "counterclaim" - i.e., each party may have a claim against the other. Usually, the goal of the mediation is to solve all disputes arising out of the same transaction, so counterclaims are considered. If the dispute arises from an ongoing transaction, such as a construction project, there may be multiple claims by a contractor against the owner. Separate mediations may be held to deal with individual claims, rather than attempting to settle all claims at the same time. However, it is more efficient to resolve as many disputes as possible in one mediation. The free flow of information in the mediation process lends itself to the resolution of multiple claims during the mediation session.

8. When do parties agree to attempt to resolve a dispute by mediation?

As mediation has gained in popularity, parties now routinely include clauses in their contracts that require them to attempt to resolve their disputes by mediation before any litigation is commenced. Some contracts require that the parties choose a mediator to serve for the duration of the contract, even before any disputes arise. Even if the contract does not contain a mediation clause, parties always have the option of agreeing to submit a dispute to mediation.

Of course, many disputes do not result from contractual agreements. Parties to any type of dispute may choose to submit to mediation. This decision may be the result of a suggestion by an attorney or one of the parties. In most cases, it is a mutual decision of the parties. However, many courts now have mandatory mediation programs which require certain cases to be submitted to mediation as part of the pre-trial process, even if the parties are not amenable to mediation. Involuntary mediation may have a lower chance of success than voluntary mediation.

9. Are all disputes susceptible to resolution by mediation?

Not all parties are amenable to having their disputes mediated. The disputes that have the highest likelihood of being resolved by mediation are those in which the parties have an ongoing relationship which they wish to maintain. The parties are therefore usually committed to resolving their dispute without resorting to litigation, and more than likely possess equal bargaining power.

For example, suppose a dispute arises between a retail seller of goods and its wholesale supplier. The parties have had an ongoing business relationship for years. A large shipment is delivered, and a majority of the goods are not those that the retailer claims it ordered. The nonconforming goods are not discovered until the goods have been in the retailer's warehouse for a month. The retailer wants to return the items for replacement, but the supplier claims that the retailer ordered the goods as delivered, and the contract states that all sales are final.

Both parties want the matter resolved quickly, and value their ongoing business relationship. Such a dispute will probably be resolved by mediation, because the parties are committed to resolving it.

Let us consider an example at the other end of the spectrum. A small business buys a computer from a computer company. After extensive business data has been loaded into the new computer, the computer crashes. Luckily, the business owner has the original data in hard copy, and immediately buys another computer. The business is severely impacted for one week while the information is loaded in the new computer.

When the business owner calls the computer company and complains, the owner of the computer company tells the business owner that "no computer I have sold has ever crashed" and the computer probably crashed because of "something your employee did while loading the computer." The business owner sues the supplier of the crashed computer for business interruption, vowing never to deal with the computer company again.

Is this dispute ripe for mediation? Possibly. Mediation may be advisable for such a highly emotional situation, if the business owner does not want to invest the time and effort to sue the computer company. However, in a situation such as this, with no ongoing relationship between the parties, and emotions running high, the business owner may decide to use the legal process rather than mediation, as he may want a decision as to fault, rather than a settlement.

Family disputes present their own opportunities for mediation. If spouses in divorce proceedings seek to end their relationship in a rational and positive way, they often choose mediation rather than litigation. On the other hand, if their goal is to inflict emotional and financial damage upon each other, they may resist any suggestion to mediate.

10. Should I suggest mediation to parties who have decided to resolve a dispute by arbitration?

If you believe the parties would be amenable to mediation, it never hurts to suggest it. When parties come to me seeking my services as an arbitrator, I will usually explore with them the possibility of mediating the dispute first. The parties may not be aware that mediation is an alternative, and they often seize the opportunity to avoid extensive costs and legal fees.

The parties may simply not be interested in mediating the dispute. I once was appointed as an arbitrator in a matter which I thought was classic for mediation - amicable parties involved in an ongoing business relationship, with a relatively small amount in dispute. When I suggested mediation, both parties politely refused. Neither party was interested in compromising its position. The dollar amount in dispute was not significant. Principle, not money, was at issue. The parties wanted to present the evidence and have the arbitrator render a binding decision on the merits.

If you have been chosen as an arbitrator, and you suggest mediation to the parties, they should choose another individual as the mediator. If you are a trained mediator, and they wish you to provide mediation services, then you would not be able to serve as the arbitrator if the mediation does not result in a settlement. Mediation requires that you meet privately with the parties and receive confidential information. An individual who has served as a mediator would then be disqualified to serve as an arbitrator, as an arbitrator is not allowed to have private, *ex parte* contact with the parties.

The Role of the
Mediator

THE ROLE OF THE MEDIATOR

11. How do the parties select a mediator?

Parties may seek candidates from administering organizations that maintain lists of qualified individuals with expertise in various fields, such as construction, computers, general business, personal injury, divorce, and family matters. Attorneys representing parties may suggest an individual with whom they are familiar and who has the requisite expertise.

12. Is it possible that more than one mediator is needed?

In complex cases the parties may want to use more than one mediator. The mediators may identify separate issues to be resolved independently, and divide these issues among themselves for attempted resolution. The mediators may also deal with issues together to aid each other in analyzing complex factual or legal scenarios. We will discuss the dynamics of "co-mediation" by more than one mediator when we discuss the actual mediation process.

13. Do I have to be an attorney in order to be a mediator?

No. Many mediators are attorneys, and many are not. Usually the parties request that the mediator be knowledgeable in the subject matter of the dispute. A mediator of family disputes may be a social worker or a psychologist. Construction disputes are often resolved by contractors, engineers, or real estate developers. Labor mediators are representatives of labor or management.

However, in some disputes, it may not be necessary for the mediator to be a specialist in any particular subject. There are some mediators who hold themselves out as generalists with expertise in various fields.

14. How can I understand legal issues if I am not an attorney?

It is the responsibility of the parties and their attorneys to present their positions so that the mediator may understand the issues in dispute. If there is a legal issue that the parties believe is critical to the case, require the parties to explain it to you, either orally or in writing. Request copies of court decisions that the parties believe are applicable, and have the parties highlight or underline the relevant facts and findings. Have the parties discuss with you why they believe these cases are similar to their dispute. These discussions may take place either in the joint session with all parties present or in private caucuses.

You should not be intimidated by legalese. Emphasize to the parties that it is their responsibility to clearly present the case to you. Continue to ask clarifying questions until you understand the parties' positions. In mediation, the complicated rules for including and excluding evidence that are used by courts are not used to filter the information presented to the mediator. Even though the rules of evidence are not used in this manner in mediation, an understanding of the basic concepts of the rules of evidence will be helpful to you. I have attempted to summarize these concepts in **Appendix C**, Everything You Never Wanted to Know about the Rules of Evidence. As you will see, these rules are based on only a handful of major concepts which can be easily understood.

15. Should the parties enter into a written agreement with me?

Yes. You should enter into a contract directly with the parties. The attorneys should not be parties to the agreement. You do not want the attorneys to pay your fees, as they are not parties to the mediation agreement nor have they retained you. The agreement should specify compensation and an agreement by the parties that they will not subpoena you as a witness in any arbitration or litigation which may occur if the mediation does not result in a settlement. I have included as **Appendix A** a sample agreement between the mediator and the parties which contains a description of the mediator's role and compensation details.

16. How do I protect myself from liability?

Some administering organizations include in their rules that neither the organization nor the mediator shall be liable for any act or omission in connection with any mediation conducted under the rules of the organization. I prefer to put the same disclaimer in my agreement with the parties (See **Appendix A**). There are various insurance carriers that provide liability coverage for mediators.

17. If I am a good arbitrator, does that mean I will be a good mediator?

Many mediators have had their introduction to alternative dispute resolution by serving as arbitrators. Compared to mediation, arbitration is a structured, passive process. The arbitrator presides over prehearing meetings and the evidentiary hearing and thereafter renders an award. The arbitrator spends most of the time listening, and less time talking.

Mediation is less structured, and the mediator is a more active participant. The personality of the mediator, as well as the mediator's ability to interact with people, may determine whether the mediation results in a settlement or not.

Now, let's answer the question. If you are a good arbitrator, you may be a good mediator, or you may not be. The skills employed in arbitration are equally applicable to mediation - listening, weighing evidence, deciding procedures to be used. However, the mediator begins the process with very little authority as compared to the arbitrator's authority to render a decision. At the beginning of the mediation process, the mediator has the limited authority to conduct the mediation, with no guarantee that the mediation will result in a settlement. Any additional authority must be earned by the mediator, by gaining the confidence of the parties as the process progresses.

Arbitration presents the arbitrator with a greater degree of control over the outcome of the resolution of the dispute. Unless a case settles before the hearing is concluded, arbitration always concludes with an award, and therefore, from the arbitrator's point of view, the outcome is within the arbitrator's control. Mediation may succeed, and it may not. Whether you will be a good mediator depends on your ability to have the parties confer authority upon you, and your ability to handle the uncertainty of the process.

18. What authority does the mediator have?

Even though the mediator does not have the authority to decide which party should prevail, the mediator does have authority to control the process and to suggest solutions. This authority is conferred upon the mediator by the parties as the mediator gains their confidence during the mediation session. We will discuss this in detail later.

19. What questions do I ask when I am appointed as the mediator?

When you are appointed as a mediator, you must inquire about the details of the dispute to determine if there are participants involved with whom you have had past contact. You need to know this in order to decide if you can serve as an impartial mediator. If you have had significant professional or social contact with any participant, you may believe that your impartiality may be affected, and you would then disqualify yourself from serving. Even if you do not believe your impartiality is affected, the parties may believe that it would be, based on your past contact, and they may request that you disqualify yourself. For example, you might ask:

Who are the parties to the dispute?

Who are the affiliates and subsidiaries of the parties?

What is the subject matter of the dispute?

Who are the major subcontractors or other interested parties involved in the dispute?

Who are the attorneys, expert witnesses and consultants that are known when the request for mediation is made?

Who are the insurance carriers for the parties?

20. What information must I disclose about myself?

You may be qualified as a mediator because of your experience in a particular industry or field. It is not uncommon for you to have had contact with many individuals in your industry. Your initial duty is to disclose any previous contacts you may have had with the participants in the mediation, whether these contacts were social or professional, regular or intermittent.

Any disclosure you make should be made in writing. Past contact and disclosure do not necessarily mean that you will be disqualified, or that you should disqualify yourself, as the mediator. As long as you and the parties are convinced that the past contact will not affect your impartiality, you should not be disqualified. If the parties do not disqualify you, they should also acknowledge your disclosure in writing. If you have any doubt as to whether you should disclose a prior contact, you should make the disclosure. Failure to disclose an innocent contact may result in an appearance of impropriety at a later date if the contact is subsequently revealed.

Preliminary Procedures

PRELIMINARY PROCEDURES

21. How do I communicate with the parties after I am appointed as the mediator?

If you have ever served as an arbitrator, you are aware that it is absolutely essential that any contact the arbitrator has with a party must be in the presence of all parties. When an arbitrator has contact with only one party, it is called *ex parte* contact. An arbitrator must avoid *ex parte* contact. The most innocent *ex parte* contact with a party can be used to discredit an arbitrator's impartiality, and may serve as a ground to *vacate* the arbitration award.

In contrast to arbitration, communications between the mediator and the parties are not restricted during the mediation session. You may have contact with one party without the other party being present. Since you are not rendering a decision, the parties should not fear that one-on-one communication between the mediator and the parties may lead to bias on the part of the mediator.

22. What should I do after I have made the necessary disclosures?

You should arrange a preliminary conference.

23. What do I discuss in the preliminary conference?

The preliminary conference can be held in person or by telephone. If the case is complex with multiple parties, you may prefer to have the preliminary conference in person. There are several reasons for holding a preliminary conference. Use it as an opportunity to introduce yourself to the parties and answer any questions concerning the mediation process.

Discuss with the parties their need to conduct discovery before the mediation begins. While parties often do not engage in extensive discovery before a mediation session, they may wish to conduct limited discovery. Also request that the parties send you a brief "premediation memorandum" describing the dispute together with selected relevant documents so that you can become familiar with the issues in dispute before the mediation begins.

Schedule the mediation in the near future. Once parties indicate a willingness to mediate a dispute, the mediation should begin as quickly as possible. Emphasize that the parties must have a representative with sufficient settlement authority present at the mediation session.

You can briefly explain the procedure that will be followed in the mediation, and inform the parties that in the "joint session" of the mediation, which is the initial meeting with the mediator and the parties, you will expect the parties to briefly present their position in an opening statement.

24. What should the parties include in their premediation memoranda?

When the parties request mediation, the mediator may not have the benefit of a document similar to a complaint in a lawsuit or an arbitration demand which summarizes the dispute between the parties. You should therefore ask each party for a premediation memorandum.

The premediation memoranda should include a brief description of the facts that gave rise to the dispute, a list of issues to be resolved, a summary of the damages claimed, and any other information which the parties believe would be helpful for you to know before the mediation begins. You should require the parties to send copies of their memoranda to each other, unless they wish to transmit confidential information to you and not share this with the other party.

25. Should I limit the length of the parties' premediation memoranda?

Yes. Unless the case is very complex, five pages is sufficient. Otherwise, you may receive a lengthy discourse which is not necessary at this stage of the mediation.

26. What documents do I need to review before the mediation?

In addition to the premediation memorandum, you should require the parties to provide you copies of selected documents which they believe are relevant to the dispute, including correspondence and the contract between the parties.

I emphasize that you should request selected documents. Unlike litigation and arbitration, you do not want to be inundated by every piece of paper that the parties consider to be relevant. As we will discuss later, you will not be poring over these documents in order to render a decision, nor will the parties need to persuade you as to the correctness of their positions. The purpose of reviewing these documents is so that you can become familiar with the background of the dispute. Do not invite the parties to submit a large volume of documents. They should be selective so that you only review documents containing information specific to the dispute.

27. What schedule should I propose for the mediation?

Many mediations are concluded in a day or less. Some only require a few hours. Some require more than a day. It is important for the mediation process to proceed with momentum towards a settlement, so you should schedule the mediation for at least a day. Resist requests to schedule the session only for a morning or afternoon.

Schedule the mediation to begin in the morning. Do not allow the distractions from the first half of the day to be brought to a mediation scheduled to begin in the afternoon. For complex cases, you should also schedule a day to reconvene, preferably the next day.

28. Should the parties bring their attorneys to the mediation?

The parties often ask if they "need to bring" their attorneys to the mediation. If a party feels the need to bring an attorney, I can not exclude the attorney, nor would I want to suggest doing so. However, depending on the attorney's understanding of the mediation process, the presence of attorneys may prove to be detrimental and counterproductive. If an attorney is a litigator and not familiar with the mediation process, that attorney may approach the process as he or she would approach litigation.

My suggestion is that there are two categories of individuals who should attend. For the purpose of understanding the dispute, there should be individuals who have personal knowledge of the facts of the dispute. Also, individuals with authority to settle the matter should attend. Attorneys are optional. If the parties feel their attorneys are necessary, I request that a party whose attorney will be present inform the other party that its counsel will be attending. You do not want one party to attend with an attorney without letting the other party know this in advance. The appearance of an attorney without notice to the other party may very well stop the mediation before it begins.

29. Why might an attorney be an impediment to mediation?

Mediation is not an adversarial process. It is a process of conciliation and compromise, in which the parties desire to settle the matter in a manner acceptable to all parties and work towards that goal. However, some attorneys do not understand, or choose not to understand, the mediation process. They act as if they were before an arbitrator or judge, trying to convince the mediator of the correctness of their client's position. Some quash all attempts at dialogue, proclaiming ultimatums and "bottom lines," or worse, discouraging their clients from accepting reasonable settlement offers, because they "could do better in litigation."

Your goal during the mediation should be to identify any person who views mediation as an adversarial procedure. You should do your utmost to educate these persons as to the nature of the mediation process.

30. What should I tell an attorney about the mediation process?

In the early '90's I found that many attorneys perceived mediation as a threat to their livelihood. A quick solution meant less billable hours. A free-flowing discussion of issues that results in a settlement and precludes months of pre-trial discovery may be wonderful for the client but disastrous to a litigator's cash flow.

Most attorneys now realize that mediation is beneficial to clients, and is another forum for the advocate. Mediation should be viewed as a step in the settlement process which occurs in all disputes. It is an opportunity for attorneys to become more actively involved in the settlement process earlier in the dispute. If mediation fails, then the case is still available for more traditional means of dispute resolution. When mediation succeeds, as if often does, the client is a satisfied client, and will return for the attorney's services in the future.

31. How can an attorney further the mediation process?

Attorneys can aid in the mediation process by candidly exploring the strengths and weaknesses of the case with their clients before the mediation begins, and actively participating with the mediator in analyzing the issues presented by all parties. There are seminars and continuing education courses on mediation advocacy. Those who have not been trained in alternative dispute resolution should arrange to take this type of training.

The attorney's demeanor in mediation should be less combative and more empathetic to the other side. I have seen attorneys in mediation greatly enhance the possibility of settlement by actively and visibly listening to the opposing party and acknowledging the distress that the opponent has incurred. An attorney can do this without conceding liability on behalf of his own client.

Another word of advice to the legal profession. During mediation, speak in plain language and avoid "legalese" as much as possible. The mediator may not be an attorney, and the opposing party may not be represented by an attorney. Communication, not intimidation, is the key requirement.

32. How do the parties prepare for mediation?

Unlike litigation or arbitration, the parties will not be required to go through a period of discovery where they gather information from the opposing party before trial or a hearing. Therefore, one of the advantages of mediation is that there is relatively little preparation before the mediation session begins. As long as the party is knowledgeable as to the facts of the dispute, it should be able to present its case effectively to the mediator. Even so, the parties may want to engage in limited discovery before the mediation. They should do so if they believe it is necessary to develop a presentation of their case.

33. If the mediation does not result in a settlement, may I then serve as an arbitrator in the same dispute?

If the mediation fails to result in a settlement, a request for the mediator to arbitrate the dispute is fairly common, as it seems to be a convenient arrangement to the parties. After all, the mediator will become educated about the dispute, even if the mediation does not result in a settlement. As convenient as this sounds, you must remember that as a mediator you are participating in settlement discussions. In the course of the mediation, it is acceptable that you have *ex parte*, private, contact with the parties and they may tell you matters in confidence. If you do so, you become aware of information you normally would not hear, nor would you be allowed to hear, as an arbitrator.

Do not rule out the possibility of becoming the arbitrator. It is possible that during the mediation nothing will occur to affect your ability to act as an arbitrator. I therefore base any decision to serve as an arbitrator on the nature of the parties' communications to me during the mediation.

I caution you before you assume the role of an arbitrator. If you have never been trained as an arbitrator, do not assume you know how to act as such. An arbitrator does not interact with the parties in the same manner as a mediator. Arbitration is a very structured method of dispute resolution. As an arbitrator, you are called upon to render a binding decision based upon a more formal presentation of information. There are specific procedures and techniques unique to the arbitration process that you should know in order to act successfully as an arbitrator.

Conducting the Mediation - Physical Setting and General Procedure

CONDUCTING THE MEDIATION -
PHYSICAL SETTING AND GENERAL PROCEDURE

34. Where should the mediation be conducted?

The most favorable location for mediation is "neutral territory" agreeable to all parties. One of the parties may suggest having the mediation at its place of business or the offices of its attorney. If you have the facilities, it is best to conduct the hearing at your place of business, rather than the place of business of a party. Having the mediation at your own office will give you more control over the process.

35. What facilities do I need?

For the initial meeting, called the "joint session," you will need a conference room large enough so that everyone can sit comfortably. You will also need a smaller room where you can meet with the parties individually during caucuses. Those not involved in the caucus may remain in the conference room.

36. What seating arrangement is used for mediation?

I prefer a round table for the joint session. A round table promotes dialogue rather than adversity, and allows me to speak directly to all participants without turning my head from side to side. Also, a round table has no corners or opposite sides. Psychologically, this round shape promotes a sense of cooperation.

If you do not have a round table, but have a rectangular table, you should sit on one side of the table facing both parties, and have the parties and their attorneys sit next to each other:

Mediator

TABLE

Attorney #1 Party #1   Party #2 Attorney #2

This arrangement keeps everyone facing you, rather than facing each other. It places the parties next to each other, and the attorneys away from the opposite party. You should also have a writing surface, such as a blackboard or sketch pad, available for people to draw diagrams.

For a multiparty mediation with many participants I prefer a long rectangular conference table. I sit at one end so that I am facing all the participants.

37. Do I always need a conference table?

In situations such as family mediation, a table is not really necessary. If the parties do not need a writing surface or a place to spread out papers, a table may foster confrontation rather than facilitate mediation. If you believe a table is not necessary, have the mediation in a room where parties can sit comfortably facing you.

38. What should be the mediator's demeanor?

A judge or arbitrator must be somewhat removed from the parties and maintain a steady "judicial" temperament. As the parties have conferred authority upon them to hear evidence and render a binding decision, the judge or arbitrator remains in a somewhat passive, non-reactive role, except to rule on objections to evidence and ask clarifying questions. The parties have the burden of proving their case, and direct their presentation to the judge or arbitrator.

On the other hand, the mediator is actively involved with the parties to the mediation. The mediator need not be convinced of the correctness of either party's position, but is there *to facilitate the communication of the parties with each other.* The mediator's stance is not "prove your case to me;" rather, it is "let me help you help each other."

The mediator should have an upbeat, positive demeanor. After all, the mediation is a positive event, is it not? The parties have decided to attempt to end their dispute by communicating with each other.

39. What is the general procedure used in mediation?

Appendix B is an outline entitled **"Stages of Mediation."** It is included as a summary of a successful mediation which results in a settlement. I suggest you refer to the appendix as you read the remainder of this book.

The mediation begins with all persons in attendance meeting in the same room for what is called the **"joint session."**

The mediator first makes an **"opening statement."** In the opening statement, the mediator introduces himself and explains the mediation process. The parties then make **"opening statements,"** explaining their respective cases. The mediator can, and usually does, ask questions, in order to clarify and define the issues, and the parties have an opportunity to ask questions of each other.

After the initial session, the mediator meets with one party privately, in a **"caucus."** Caucuses are usually held in a smaller room, possibly the mediator's office. The party not meeting with the mediator may be left in the conference room where the joint session was held, or may wait in another room. During the caucus, the mediator discusses the party's case, asking the party questions, and explores the strengths and weaknesses of the case. The discussions are confidential, and the mediator cannot reveal the contents of these discussions to the other party unless authorized.

The mediator then holds a caucus with the other party and confidentially explores its case. The caucuses continue, as the mediator moves back and forth between the parties. As the result of the mediator's probing the parties' positions, the mediator develops an understanding of the areas of agreement and disagreement. At some point, the parties tell the mediator in confidence their compromise positions. The mediator then discovers the negotiating range established by the parties.

Eventually, a party may authorize the mediator to transmit a settlement offer to the other party. At this point, the process evolves from analysis of the dispute to negotiations. Settlement offers may be transmitted back and forth until a settlement is reached. If most issues are resolved, but only one or two remain that appear unresolvable, the mediator may suggest that the parties meet again in a joint session and speak directly to each other.

Once a settlement agreement has been reached, the mediator should have the parties draft an agreement in writing. As discussed later, the mediator does not draft the settlement agreement. This agreement need not be a fully developed legal document, as the parties may wish their attorneys to draft the final agreement. However, at a minimum, the mediator should attempt to have the parties write down the points of agreement, so there will be no dispute as to exactly what has been agreed.

The final stage is often referred to as **"closure."** This is a joint meeting in which the parties review the settlement agreement to assure that no issues remain unresolved. The mediator commends the parties for resolving the matter, and the mediation is concluded.

40. Who is allowed in the mediation session?

Court proceedings are generally a matter of public record and open to the public. Mediation is confidential. The parties and their attorneys are allowed in the mediation session. Allowances are made for necessary persons, such as those who will serve as expert witnesses or consultants aiding in the presentation or preparation of a party's case. In family mediation or divorce mediation, the participants often want friends or relatives to be present for emotional support. If a party feels the presence of friends is absolutely necessary, then the mediator may allow these individuals to attend.

During private caucuses, you may request to speak with the attorney without the client, or the client without the attorney. Experts or consultants may be included only during certain portions of the mediation.

41. May I exclude parties or other persons from the room?

If you have issues you wish to discuss in private with certain individuals, you should suggest that others allow you the privacy to discuss these issues. There are times that you may want to have a discussion with a party's attorney, or both attorneys, without the parties present, or a party or both parties without attorneys present. It is helpful to have a "break out" room for such discussions.

Feel free to suggest such discussions. The parties or the attorneys may welcome the chance to speak with you in private. I have had instances where the attorneys met with me privately and told me that they had both recommended a reasonable settlement but the parties were being stubborn. I have also experienced the reverse situation, where the parties have informed me that they were willing to settle but their attorneys were encouraging them to continue to negotiate for a better deal. Sometimes an attorney's fee agreement is the sticking point. An attorney working on a contingent fee may encourage the client towards a larger settlement in order to maximize the fee. Without commenting on the ethics of this situation, I can assure you I have seen this happen. I found myself involved in a brief subsidiary mediation between the attorney and client to modify the fee arrangement.

42. What should I do if for the first time at the mediation I recognize a participant that I know?

Immediate disclosure is required if you recognize someone. You should inform the parties of your past contact with the individual and state whether you believe your past contact will affect your impartiality. Obviously, if you think your impartiality has been affected, you will have to withdraw as the mediator. Usually, immediate disclosure and your statement that your impartiality would not be affected is sufficient for the parties to waive any objection to your past contact.

43. How do I avoid improper contact with the participants during the mediation?

Ex parte contact is allowed during mediation. The danger in mediation is that one party may hear discussions that are only intended to be heard by the other party. Have private conversations behind closed doors, not in hallways or elevators. Be careful what you say in the restroom. You never know who may be in there or who may walk in while you are there. Your fellow employees may know that a mediation is taking place in the office, and ask you questions as to how it is going if they happen to see you outside the hearing room. Your best response is no response. The mediation should not be a topic of general discussion at your place of business, as the proceedings are confidential.

Do not accept rides from or offer transportation to any of the participants. If you have the mediation at your office, this is usually not an issue. Remember - even though private contact is acceptable behavior during the mediation session, you still must avoid appearances of partiality to any party.

44. What if one party is represented by an attorney and the other is not?

Problems arise when a party brings counsel unexpectedly, and the other party states that had this been known, its counsel would have come also. A party who intends for its attorney to attend should inform the other party in advance of the mediation.

You should inquire during the preliminary conference whether the parties will have their attorneys attend the mediation. If a party is not certain, you should ask that you and the other party be informed once the decision is made whether counsel will attend.

45. Does mediation require a court reporter and a transcript of the proceedings?

Mediation is essentially a settlement discussion. As such, anything said during the mediation process is inadmissible in court. There is no need for a court reporter or a transcript of the proceedings. Anyone who demands that a court reporter be present to transcribe the proceedings either does not understand the purpose of the process or wishes to use the process for something other than its intended purpose.

46. Should I take notes during the mediation?

Whether you take notes depends on your personal preference. I find it helpful in order to frame my own questions. If there are several issues, notes help me to remember who has spoken on a given topic. Some mediators have told me that they prefer not to take notes, as note taking detracts from their ability to listen to the parties' presentations. I have found that I take detailed notes in the negotiation phase to assure that I have accurately understood settlement offers .

Some mediators take notes with a laptop computer. I have found that parties may relate this to a court reporter making a record of the proceedings. They actually may speak slowly so that the mediator types exactly what is said. I have seen a party ask the mediator to "read back" what they have said. You should be careful not to create an impression that you are making a detailed record of every word spoken during the mediation session.

Always take your notes with you when you leave the room. Do not leave them on the table for anyone to see, or for someone to pick up by mistake.

47. Should I ask permission to take notes?

Everything said in the mediation is confidential. I therefore ask the parties' permission to take notes. I emphasize that my taking notes will help me function more effectively as a mediator, and that I use my notes as a safeguard to make sure I have understood the parties' positions, as well as to accurately relay offers of settlement. I have never had anyone object to my taking notes. I assure the parties that I will destroy the notes after the mediation is concluded.

48. Why should I inform the parties that I will destroy my notes?

I always make a point of informing the parties that I will destroy my notes at the end of the mediation. This serves several purposes. The parties know that confidentiality will be preserved. They also know that there will be no physical evidence of what transpired during the mediation. For your own protection, let it be known that once the mediation is concluded, no written evidence of the proceedings will exist.

Destroy your notes immediately after the mediation session. My standard agreement with the parties contains a condition that the parties will not attempt to subpoena me or my notes in subsequent litigation. In the event that a party violates this condition of the agreement and attempts to subpoena your notes in subsequent litigation, you will not have anything to produce in response to the subpoena if you have destroyed your notes immediately after the mediation is concluded.

If you have not destroyed your notes, and you do receive a subpoena, you cannot then destroy your notes but must produce them in accordance with the subpoena. The fact that the parties have violated their agreement with you not to subpoena your notes does not relieve you of the obligation to comply with the subpoena.

49. Is there anything I should not do during a mediation?

Do not allow yourself to be constantly interrupted to take care of other business during the mediation. While some interruptions are inevitable, you need to give the mediation your full attention, and should not be preoccupied with other matters. This caveat also applies to the participants. They should arrange their schedules to avoid interruptions during the mediation.

50. What is co-mediation?

The parties may request more than one mediator to resolve complex disputes. Co-mediation is the use of two or more mediators in a single mediation proceeding. Once the issues are identified, the mediators may divide the issues and meet separately with the parties to discuss their assigned issues. The parties may designate individuals to deal with the specific groups of issues, so that two mediations proceed simultaneously with the mediators and their respective party groups. Alternatively, the two mediators may work together to evaluate the same issues.

The Joint Session -
The Mediator's
Opening Statement

THE JOINT SESSION -
THE MEDIATOR'S OPENING STATEMENT

51. What is the purpose of the mediator's opening statement?

The purpose of your opening statement is to educate the participants as to your role as mediator, what mediation is, and how mediation works.

The opening statement has another, more subtle purpose. You use your opening statement to begin to establish your authority in the process. Remember, you have no authority to impose a solution. So what authority do you have? We'll see in a few minutes.

52. How do I explain the mediator's role and the mediation process in my opening statement?

Parties and attorneys often come to the mediation with incorrect perceptions of the role of the mediator and the mediation process. Some expect a mediator to act like a judge or an arbitrator and make rulings that bind the parties. Having chosen mediation as the means to possibly resolve the dispute, the parties still may not understand that mediation is a process which places the burden on *them* to agree to a resolution of the dispute.

Your opening statement provides an opportunity to explain your role and the mediation process. It could be similar to the following:

Welcome to mediation. I am _____. [Briefly describe your background]

I look forward to the opportunity to help you resolve the dispute at hand. Let me take a few moments to explain my role as the mediator. I am neither a judge nor an arbitrator. You have not conferred upon me the authority to decide which party will prevail in this dispute or determine an amount of monetary recovery. Instead, I am here to help you resolve the dispute.

Mediation is not an adversarial process. You are not here to convince me that your position is right and the other party is wrong. Rather, we are here to discuss the strengths and weaknesses of your positions, and hopefully arrive at a mutually agreed settlement. If you were in court, you would be directing your presentation to the judge. In mediation, I urge you to listen to each other, and speak to each other.

We will start with an opening presentation from each side. I will ask questions so that I can fully understand the positions of both parties. Then I will meet in private with each party. Anything that is said in mediation is confidential. Because mediation is a structured settlement process, anything you say to each other or to me is not admissible in court. Therefore, please speak freely.

As a mediator, you have an opportunity to work on your opening statement and improve it as you become more experienced. Based upon the nature of the dispute and the parties knowledge of the process, you will revise your opening statement to fit the situation at hand.

53. What authority does the mediator have?

The mediator does not have the authority to render a decision and decide the outcome of the dispute. In fact, you may have noticed that I have emphasized this lack of authority in my opening statement above. However, to say that the mediator has no authority in the process is not true. The mediator's authority is subtle, and must be earned from the parties. *The authority that the mediator must earn is the authority to control the process and be trusted by both parties.*

Whatever authority the mediator has rests in his or her ability to appeal to the parties to settle the dispute and the parties' recognition of the mediator's ability to guide them in this effort. As such, the authority of the mediator is actually granted by the parties to the mediator as the mediation progresses. By remaining impartial and gaining the trust of the parties, the parties come to trust the suggestions and solutions posed by the mediator, and ultimately the mediator may influence the outcome of the dispute.

54. How do I begin to establish authority?

Your opening statement is your first opportunity to establish your authority to control the process and to gain the parties' trust. You should briefly describe your background and expertise in the subject matter:

Example 1:

For the past fifteen years, I have been a general contractor and a subcontractor. I have been both a plaintiff in lawsuits and a defendant. I know what it is like to be involved in a dispute like this. Regardless of the resolution of the dispute, you will benefit by resolving the matter as quickly as possible.

Example 2:

For the past ten years, I have been a lawyer practicing employment law. I have represented both employers and employees in situations such as this. I am familiar with the legal issues in such disputes. I have successfully resolved similar disputes by mediation. It certainly is less costly and more satisfactory to the parties to resolve the dispute in this manner. I welcome the opportunity to help you resolve your dispute today.

Example 3:

I have been a social worker for five years. During that time I have dealt with approximately 300 cases of ongoing family problems. I have seen the problems and the pain caused by divorce. I have also mediated more than 50 marital disputes. While it may not be accurate to talk in terms of winners and losers when it comes to family disputes, the benefits of mediation are that a resolution is certainly less costly and less stressful than resolving your problems in court.

55. Should I describe my background in detail?

No, be rather brief. The parties will already know the details of your background, having picked you as the mediator. More than likely they contacted you initially and requested your resume. Your background is relevant in the opening statement to show that you have experience in the subject matter and empathy for the parties, since you have worked in the same industry. A short chronological summary should suffice.

The Joint Session - The Parties' Opening Statements

THE JOINT SESSION -
THE PARTIES' OPENING STATEMENTS

56. How do the parties present their opening statements?

In your premediation conference with the parties, you advised them that they were required to present an opening statement during the joint session. A party's opening statement may be presented by the party, its attorney, or by both. The party can state the facts of the dispute and the attorney can offer legal interpretation. While the mediator may suggest that the party take an active role, you cannot and should not attempt to compel a party to participate actively if the attorney does not wish the party to do so.

57. Why do some mediator's consider the parties' opening statements the most important part of the mediation process?

As a dispute develops and the parties invest emotional and financial resources, their ultimate desire is to have their "day in court" so that they may tell a decision maker their story. If the dispute goes to litigation, the parties become involved in discovery procedures and other pretrial matters, and it is often months or years before the parties have the opportunity to deal with anyone other than each other and their attorneys.

The parties' opening statements in mediation have great therapeutic value. They are allowed to tell their story and vent their concerns to the mediator early in the dispute resolution process. Making the opening statement provides a visible catharsis. Even though the mediator is not a decision maker like a judge or arbitrator, you can see a burden lifted from the parties as they complete their opening statements. They have finally told someone other than their attorney their side of the dispute. Having told their story, their stance shifts into what I call "settlement mode." Now they are ready to resolve the dispute.

58. What can I learn from the parties' demeanor in the joint session?

You should scrutinize the parties' demeanor very carefully during their opening statements. You can use their demeanor as a barometer for measuring the difficulty of settling the dispute. If parties characterize each other as deceitful and untrustworthy, you then realize that much of the damage that has occurred has been emotional as well as economic. On the other hand, if the parties treat each other with respect, and you sense a willingness to settle the dispute, your task will probably not be as difficult.

The attorneys' demeanor will also determine the difficulty of your task. I have seen attorneys do more harm than good during opening statements, by offering disparaging remarks about the other party. A combative stance may be the attorney's stock in trade, but it often creates impediments to settlement in the mediation process.

59. Is there another way to begin the mediation session?

Some mediators prefer to question the parties in order to define the issues, rather then allowing the parties to make their own presentations. This approach provides the mediator with an opportunity to control the process at an earlier stage, and lends a more structured approach to defining the issues.

Another approach is to forego opening statements and have the mediator state his or her understanding of the parties' positions based upon prior review of the premediation submissions and discussions the mediator has had with the parties before the mediation begins. I have used this approach in several mediations in which the parties' relationship has been particularly strained. In these situations, the parties have told me that they would rather not be in each other's presence. While they were willing to negotiate a settlement with the help of a mediator, they did not want to make presentations to each other. Instead, I took the opportunity to state my understanding of the parties' positions in the presence of the parties and allowed the parties to clarify my understanding. In this way they did not have to address each other, but were allowed to hear their positions stated based upon my understanding.

60. What are the advantages and disadvantages of allowing the parties to make opening statements?

By requiring the parties to make opening statements, rather than beginning the mediation by asking the parties questions, you run the risk of gathering disjointed information as the result of the emotional state of the parties. You may hear excessive demands, and have to bear the brunt of posturing by both the parties and their attorneys. However, I believe having the parties make opening statements is still the most effective method of beginning the mediation. By "letting it all hang out" during the joint session, you allow the parties to vent their frustration and emotion before you begin to structure the issues and meet with the parties privately.

61. How do I distinguish between argument and fact?

In litigation and arbitration, opening statements and closing arguments are generally made by attorneys. Keep in mind that attorneys are not witnesses. They were not involved in the events that have given rise to the dispute and therefore have no personal knowledge of the facts and circumstances. They are not offering testimony. They frame the facts in argumentative terms in order to present the facts in a light most favorable to their clients. That is what they are trained to do and that is what clients pay them to do.

In mediation, parties may or may not be represented by attorneys. What they say may be a mix of argumentative and factual statements.

You should not accept argumentative statements at face value without requesting factual support. Remember, your duty is to probe the viability of the parties' cases as to strengths and weaknesses.

62. How do I react to the parties' opening statements?

First and foremost, you have to *listen and understand* the positions of the parties. Not only must you listen and understand, but you should also *clarify* whatever is not clear to you.

Empathize with the parties. As an impartial mediator, be sure to empathize equally with all parties.

63. What can I do if I believe an opening statement is too long or too detailed?

A long and detailed opening statement can destroy the "let's get this resolved" momentum that you are trying to create. It can also create negative adversarial feelings if one party believes the other is trying to monopolize the proceedings. This does not happen often, but when it does you must be very diplomatic.

If you believe a party is extending the opening statement unnecessarily, you could make a suggestion such as the following:

Mr./Ms ___, I realize there are many issues in dispute, and you have your own interpretation of the facts in this matter. The purpose of our upcoming caucus is for me to spend time alone with each party and examine the details in depth. With this in mind, if you could perhaps shorten your opening statement by summarizing the remainder we can explore the details in our first caucus.

64. What comments do I make at the close of the parties' opening statements?

Your reaction to the parties' opening statements should be very positive and laudatory. Thank the parties for clearly setting forth their positions, and tell them that "we are now going to begin to work together to seek a solution to the problem." I find this type of phraseology very important at this stage. During litigation, the parties use their opening statements to state their positions so that the judge or jury can begin to determine fault. The trial proceeds with the purpose of determining the party at fault and the parties' positions are inflexible. Mediation, on the other hand, proceeds to find a mutual solution rather than determining blame.

65. What if a party brings voluminous documentation to the mediation session?

The parties may want to bring all their records as a "security blanket." They would rather have their information available in case they need it. Bringing boxes of records to the mediation is fine, as long as the parties do not expect you to look at every document. When I see parties wheeling hand trucks of documents into the conference room, I usually say something like "I hope somebody here can summarize all of that so we're not sitting here for the next three days."

On the other hand, if a party begins to prolong its opening statement by reviewing document after document you should politely caution the party that such detail is not necessary and a summary of the facts would be more appropriate. You can advise the party that you will have the opportunity to review the most important documents during the private caucus.

I was involved in a mediation where an attorney insisted on discussing every document, despite my diplomatic requests for summarization. Finally, his client took the hint and summarized the situation in about five minutes. I suppose this attorney only knew how to discuss every single piece of paper as if he were entering data into a computer. The insistence upon focusing upon every document indicates a general misperception of the process, in that the person doing so is attempting to prove the case rather than summarize the essence of the case for negotiation purposes.

Accepted courtroom tactics do not necessarily translate into efficient mediation.

The most extreme instance of voluminous documentation I encountered involved a dispute in which the parties suggested the mediation be conducted at the site of the dispute, because one party had an *entire floor* with file cabinets filled with documents. The dispute involved contract performance that had been ongoing for ten years, and I had no doubt that there was an entire floor of documents. However, I told the parties that there was nothing I could do with that many documents. They would have to select the documents most relevant to the dispute. If they could not do that, they certainly would not be prepared for mediation.

66. What do I need to accomplish in the joint session?

Your goal in the joint session is to identify all the issues that need to be resolved in order to settle the dispute. By the time the joint session is concluded, I like to have a list of issues to use as an agenda for discussion in the caucuses to follow.

Identifying issues is easier said than done. The parties' opening statements may be emotional, unorganized, stream of consciousness presentations in which the issues are not clearly defined. Issues may be created that are not necessarily significant, but are floated as "throwaway" issues to be conceded in negotiation. If the issues are not clear to you, ask the parties clarifying questions in order to identify the issues. Having done this, you now have an agenda for discussion.

67. How do I make sure I understand the parties' opening statements?

There are various methods to check your understanding of the parties' opening statements. I like to paraphrase what I believe the parties have told me. I preface my remarks by saying:

It is important that I clearly understand what you have said. Let me state what I believe you have said in my own words, and please feel free to correct me if I have misinterpreted anything you have said.

If a number of issues have been discussed, I will read my list of issues, with a short summary of each, and seek the approval of the parties as to the completeness of my list. Sometimes I will divide an issue into sub-issues for clarity. I ask questions. Depending on the circumstances, I will either ask my clarification questions during the joint session or wait until the private caucus.

68. Should I rank the issues in the order of importance?

I prefer to ask the parties to rank the issues in the order of importance. I do this during the first private caucus with each party. The parties may have a differing view of the priority of the issues. Only after you have asked the parties to rank the issues will you have a clear idea as to the actual order of importance. If one party feels that an issue is not so important, and the other party feels that it is very important, resolving this issue first may result in a quicker resolution of the entire dispute.

The First Private
Caucus

THE FIRST PRIVATE CAUCUS

69. What happens in the first private caucus?

The private caucus sets mediation apart from litigation and arbitration. After the joint session, the mediator meets with the parties in private caucus, continues the fact-finding phase and frankly discusses the strengths and weaknesses of each party's case. There may be instances in which you conduct a mediation without a private caucus. My experience is that these instances are rare.

Your goal in the first private caucus is to allow each party to continue the venting process begun in the joint session. You are free to probe the factual basis of the party's case, the strength of potential testimony, and the support the party will bring to bear if the case proceeds to trial. The party is free to tell you confidential information which it has never told the other party, to allow you to assess the case.

70. Should I have the parties rank the issues in the order of importance?

Yes. This is a very useful exercise. When you ask the parties to rank the issues in the order of importance, they will often rank the same issues in a different order. You may find that monetary issues are a primary concern to one party, while issues concerning a continuing business relationship may be the ultimate focus for the other party.

What is important to one party may be inconsequential to the other. In fact, an important issue to one party may actually be a throw-away issue to the other. An issue that both parties initially rank as important may actually be a throw-away issue for both. Identifying throw-away issues will save everyone time by reserving these issues until later, and hasten the resolution of the dispute. We will talk about throw-away issues shortly.

71. How does it help the parties to divulge confidential information?

Divulging confidential information during the private caucus is what I call "step 2" in the venting process that began when the party delivered its opening statement. Having achieved an emotional release by telling its story to the mediator and the other party, the party now has your attention in the private caucus.

Suppose that the party tells you that a portion of its damages, which it believes was fairly calculated, cannot be supported by documentation. The records supporting this part of the calculation were lost when the party moved its office last month. Having revealed this weakness in its case, you may point out that while you do not question the integrity of the party, the other party could color this lack of documentation as a "convenient disappearance," raising questions as to the credibility of the claim for damages.

Discussion of confidential information allows you to shed some reality on a party's case and to deflate a party's unrealistic expectations of success, thereby facilitating settlement.

72. What questions should I ask in the first private caucus?

In addition to allowing the parties to continue to "vent," the first private caucus is a continuation of the fact-finding procedure you used in the joint session. You should explore the factual basis of the party's claim. One helpful technique is to play "devil's advocate," and assume the role of the other party. Before doing so, you should explain to the party that you will be doing the same with the other party, so your questions should not be interpreted as bias against the party being questioned. "Devil's advocate" is merely a method of exploring the validity and logic of a party's position.

Suppose the dispute involves the interpretation of a certain contract clause. You meet in caucus with the party. During his opening statement, the party has given his interpretation of the contract clause. Your questions may be similar to the following:

Did you read the entire contract before you signed it?

Did you have an opportunity to negotiate changes to the contract before you signed it?

Did you form an understanding of the particular clause before you signed the contract?

When did you form an understanding of the contract clause?

Does the other party's interpretation sound reasonable to you?

Do you think the contract can be reasonably interpreted in more than one way or just one way?

Suppose the party says he had an opportunity to negotiate changes in the contract language. He had read the contract before he signed it, and noticed that the particular clause in question could be interpreted in two ways. In fact, he realized that if a dispute were to arise in the future, he could take advantage of the ambiguous language. Quite frankly, he admits his own interpretation is "stretching it" a bit, but it is the only language in the contract he could construe in his favor. He can see how the other party is able to interpret the contract in a favorable manner.

The party may not readily admit all of the facts we have stated above, but let's assume that after some discussion, you have elicited this information.

73. How do I inform a party of a weakness in its case?

Let's continue our example from the previous question. You should caution the party that you are not passing judgement, but based upon what he has told you, there is a definite weakness in his case.

The party was aware of an obvious ambiguity in the contract which it knew could be interpreted in the other party's favor. Knowing this, instead of clarifying the language during negotiations, the party chose to leave it ambiguous. Generally, one has a duty to clarify obvious ambiguities before signing a contract, and cannot knowingly take advantage of such ambiguities.

You may then point out to the party that a judge or arbitrator may not look with favor upon its actions, assuming this information is revealed at trial or during arbitration. In this manner, you are using your ability to predict a negative reaction in another forum to emphasize the weakness in the party's case.

At this point, you still do not know the other party's position. The other party may also have realized the ambiguity and planned to use the ambiguity to its advantage.

74. If it appears that there is an important question or an issue that both parties are avoiding, should I ask the question or raise the issue?

Absolutely! If you think it is important, ask the question or raise the issue. Do so in the private caucus, rather than jointly with all parties present. The answer to the question or the reaction to the issue might reveal a weakness in the case of one or both parties. You can only be effective if you are fully informed. Of course, the parties may choose not to answer the question or discuss the issue. You should probe as to the reasons why they do not want to address this subject.

75. What if a party fails to answer my question in a private caucus?

Don't jump to conclusions. The party may not have understood your question, or the party's emotional state may be blocking the response. Try and assess the party's state of mind before you do something which might cause anger or embarrassment. First, ask the party if he understood the question. Try and rephrase the question. Perhaps you asked a question that required the party to justify his actions (why did you do ___?), when a more objective question would be appropriate (how did __ happen?).

It could be that you have not gained the party's trust, or that the party feels it is too soon in the process to reveal the answer to the question. If you sense that the party is withholding information, refrain from asking that question again until later in the caucus.

76. How do I get past a party's certainty?

Let's face it - sometimes a party knows it has a better position than the other party. After the parties give their opening statements, a party may be more certain that it has the better position. In fact, you may be of the same opinion. In the private caucus, the party may tell you that it believes the other party has a very weak case, and there is no apparent reason to compromise a case which is a "sure winner." How do you respond?

You can emphasize that "sure winners" are rare and are usually fantasies in the minds of litigants, not realities in the minds of judges.

You can then remind the party that there is a cost to continuing a dispute, even one when one party believes he will ultimately prevail. The value of resolving a dispute may be worth more than the cost of prolonging the dispute. Urge that the mediation continue, as the party has nothing to lose in finding out what compromise, if any, could be reached . There is always a possibility that a settlement can be reached.

77. What are hidden agenda items and why are they important?

All parties come to the negotiating table with emotional baggage. Hidden agenda items are issues that are obstacles to the resolution of the dispute that the parties may not readily acknowledge as important. It is helpful for the mediator to investigate the extent of the parties' past dealings and the barriers to settlement that the relationship may have created. Resolving such hidden agenda items allows the mediation to move forward. You should be on guard to recognize such issues, as they often lead to a solution.

I was once involved in a mediation arising from a construction project in which the contractor constantly referred to the owner's failure to address other claims which the contractor had submitted months before. While these claims were not of the same magnitude as the dispute with which we were dealing in the mediation, it was apparent to me that the owner's putting these claims on the "back burner" had clouded the contractor's objectivity and willingness to deal with the owner. The owner made a reasonable settlement offer in the mediation, and yet the contractor felt that a counteroffer was not warranted, because the owner was still refusing to deal with the prior claims.

During a private caucus with the owner, I explained the contractor's reluctance to move forward with the mediation because of the mistrust created by the owner's failure to deal promptly with the other claims. The owner offered a firm commitment to address the other claims in the very near future, and included this commitment in the settlement offer. The willingness to address the previously submitted claims broke the impasse in the mediation.

78. What are throw-away issues and why are they important?

Throw-away issues are those which are inconsequential to an ultimate settlement. These are issues that a party will not pursue if other issues are resolved. The party continues to assert throw-away issues until a settlement is proposed which makes the settlement of the throw-away issues unnecessary.

For example, if a party has a series of itemized claims, there may be low dollar amount items that are throw-away issues. I try to identify a party's throw-away issues in the first private caucus and agree not to spend time discussing these issues until after the other issues are resolved. I do not characterize the issues as throw-away, but as low priority. When the major issues are resolved, the throw-away issues are usually "thrown away," as they are withdrawn by the parties because they are not worth the time and effort to resolve.

For their own reasons, parties may initially not acknowledge that certain issues are throw-away. They may wish to retain these issues for negotiating purposes. Do not be afraid to probe each issue to determine whether it must be decided in order to resolve the dispute.

79. What if a party seeks legal advice from me during the mediation session?

The mediator who is an attorney is vulnerable to requests to render legal advice or an opinion as to the merits of the parties' positions. This request sometimes is made jointly by the parties. A mediator serving as a facilitative mediator should not render an opinion on the merits of the parties' claims.

To emphasize your role as a facilitative mediator, your response may be similar to the following:

I can't give you a legal opinion as to your case. You are free to seek legal advice from your attorneys. My function is not to advise either party as to the merits of its position, but to help you settle the dispute. Besides, my legal opinion is not even relevant, because I have no authority to decide the case, nor can I predict the outcome of the case if it were to be litigated in court.

The request for a legal opinion may come from one party during a private caucus. I once was involved in a mediation with a party who tried everything to torpedo the process. His tactic was to insist that the other side had no intention of settling. Finally, he issued an ultimatum that unless I went to the other party and told them that it was my opinion that "he was right," the mediation was over. I told him that the mediation was over, because that was not my function, and I was not about to do that. I asked him to go inform the other party that the mediation was terminated. He stopped insisting on my legal opinion at that point, and the mediation continued.

The parties may jointly request a nonbinding opinion from you. They should be made aware that there is another form of alternative dispute resolution, known as "neutral case evaluation," in which the parties present their positions to a neutral person who then renders a nonbinding "advisory opinion." This is similar to nonbinding arbitration, except that the case evaluator does not hear testimony and review evidence in a hearing, but listens to a summary presentation similar to the parties' opening statements in mediation.

There also is a process known as "evaluative" mediation, in which the mediator does in fact give the parties a nonbinding opinion. The mediator is specifically requested to perform an "evaluative" mediation by the parties. The first phase of the mediation consists of fact finding sufficient to allow the mediator to render a nonbinding opinion. The mediator continues to mediate once the nonbinding opinion is given.

Attorneys and Evidentiary Concepts

ATTORNEYS AND EVIDENTIARY CONCEPTS

80. How do I deal with a hostile attorney?

Attorney hostility is difficult to define. The task of zealously representing a client lends itself to vigorous actions. Attorneys in their zeal may become counterproductive to the orderly exchange of ideas during mediation.

Attorneys bickering with each other can be stopped by suggesting a short recess to allow them to work out their differences. This usually brings the bickering to a halt, as it is a signal from you that you do not care to listen to it. Once you note your displeasure, the bickering should stop.

81. Will attorneys make objections during the mediation session?

Objections are a common practice in litigation and arbitration, but not in mediation. During these procedures, objections to testimony and written evidence are made in order to assure that the evidence in the record upon which a judge, jury, or arbitrator bases a decision or verdict is authentic, relevant, and credible. While a party or an attorney may object to statements made during the mediation, you are neither creating a record nor making a decision.

Even though you do not have to resolve objections, it is helpful for you to be familiar with the fundamental principles of evidence, in order to assess the testimony of the parties and to understand the basic terminology that attorneys use. I have included **Appendix C**, entitled "Everything You Never Wanted to Know About the Rules of Evidence," that contains a discussion of evidentiary concepts.

82. Does the person who wrote the document have to be present at the mediation session?

In mediation, it is not necessary to verify every fact by the submission of witness testimony or by documentation. If a document is relied upon by a party to illustrate a point, the author does not have to be present to verify the document's authenticity. However, if the author of an important document is no longer employed by a party, or otherwise unavailable, the party should realize this is a weakness in its case in the event the matter proceeds to arbitration or litigation.

83. Are summaries of documents submitted in mediation?

Summaries of voluminous documentation may be used to prove a point in mediation. The party offering the summary should describe the underlying documentation and establish the method used to compile the summary. If financial information is summarized, the party may offer a statement from an accountant or financial officer describing the preparation of the financial information and establishing the summary's reliability.

It is important that you realize a summary is merely a convenient means of illustrating large amounts of information. A party cannot challenge the accuracy of a summary unless it has been given the opportunity to review the underlying information. While a party in litigation and arbitration usually has the opportunity to review the opposing party's documentation before the hearing begins, this is not necessarily true in mediation.

The Second Private Caucus and Beyond - Achieving Settlement

THE SECOND PRIVATE CAUCUS AND BEYOND - ACHIEVING SETTLEMENT

84. How do the parties move toward settlement?

After clarifying the issues and ranking them in the parties' order of priority in the first caucus, you should use the second caucus to explore an initial settlement offer. Preface the discussion by stating that you will not transmit any settlement offers unless authorized. State that you would like to "begin to explore settlement options" and gain an initial overview of the party's willingness to settle. The party then reveals its initial settlement offer, but does not authorize you to transmit it to the other party. Repeat this procedure in the second caucus with the other party. After the second caucus with both parties, you now know their initial settlement offers, but they have no idea as to each other's offer.

You may be surprised by the initial settlement offers. The claimant may reduce its claim drastically, and the other party may state an offer believing it to be low, not realizing its offer is close to the claimant's offer, or at least "in the ball park." Conversely, the claimant may not reduce his claim substantially in its first offer, but the other party may propose an offer close to the claimant's original claim amount. The more typical scenario is that the claimant reduces his claim slightly for the initial offer, and the other party makes a much lower offer.

If the positions are reasonably close, the dispute will probably settle quickly. However, if the positions are far apart, you should not be discouraged, as a disparity in settlement offers is not uncommon in the initial stages. Parties tend to make substantial compromises in the negotiating phase and will usually create a negotiating range which is more realistic and conducive to settlement. As the mediator assesses strengths and weaknesses of the parties' positions the negotiating range will narrow.

85. How are settlement offers transmitted?

After the second caucus with both parties, you know the initial settlement offers, but they have not authorized you to transmit the offers. You may begin the third caucus by telling each party the following:

I have inquired as to the initial settlement offers from both parties. Neither of you have authorized me to transmit a settlement offer, but I can tell you that at this point the difference in your positions is [not very large, large, extremely large]. At this point, I believe it would beneficial to transmit your settlement offers to each other, and begin the negotiation process. Do you have any objections to doing so?

At this point, the mediation has entered a new phase.

The first fact-finding phase is for the purpose of gathering information and clarifying the interests and positions of the parties. This is accomplished in the joint session and the first caucus, which allow the parties to vent their emotion and frustration. These stages also provide the opportunity for the mediator to require the parties to prioritize the issues.

In the second caucus, the parties focus turns away from their past history and towards the resolution of the dispute, with the formulation of initial settlement offers. The third caucus begins the **negotiation stage**, where the parties authorize you to transmit settlement offers.

86. How do the parties finally reach agreement?

When the parties authorize you to transmit settlement offers, usually by the third or fourth caucus, the negotiation phase begins. You present the settlement offers, and ask for reaction. You may see posturing and bluffing, feigned insult and dismay. Do not be satisfied with emotional reactions. Probe for a more rational response. Ask for counteroffers. Seek other solutions. Discuss previously identified hidden agenda items. The goal at this point is to create momentum towards settlement. Any movement, no matter how slight, is all that it takes to keep the momentum moving forward. You can encourage further movement by making statements similar to the following:

I know this offer may be disappointing to you, but it is not the final offer. What counteroffer can you make?

At least this represents some movement. If you can, make a counteroffer and see what response you get.

What do you think an appropriate response should have been?

What response would you need, not necessarily to resolve this, but at least to keep you at the table?

87. How do I deal with a party who does not have a representative present with settlement authority?

Even though you have emphasized to the parties that their representatives must come to the mediation session with sufficient settlement authority, a mediation may come to a sudden halt if a party representative does not have sufficient authority to settle the dispute. This may not be discovered until the final bargaining stage, when the offers that are transmitted are outside the range of a party representative's authority to accept.

Your immediate reaction when you discern a lack of settlement authority should be to have the party seek settlement authority. A phone call to the proper person may be all that is needed. However, settlement authority may not be immediately forthcoming. The party may have a

Board of Directors or other governing body which has to approve the settlement. Your efforts should be directed at having the party acquire settlement authority before the other party discovers that it is dealing with someone who lacks authority.

88. What can I do if the negotiations reach an impasse?

An impasse can occur for many reasons. The parties may be exhausted and simply not have the energy to continue. They may have come to the limit of their authority to settle without a resolution. Their expectations for a quick settlement may have been disappointed and they may feel they need time to think about the matter.

Defuse the impasse. If it is late in the day, suggest a recess until the next morning and schedule a time to reconvene. By this point the parties probably need time to consult their attorneys and digest what they have heard. You can suggest that the parties have dinner with each other. Relaxation in a comfortable environment may lead to a resolution to continue the mediation.

You should be aware that even a minor issue may become insurmountable as the parties become tired and lose perspective. You can avoid the impasse by suggesting that the parties reserve discussion of that particular issue until other issues are decided. By the time you focus on the issue again, other issues have been resolved and the parties negotiating momentum may resolve what once seemed insurmountable.

I have been quite surprised in instances where the parties were completely stymied at the end of the day and have returned the next day to continue as if there had been no impasse the previous day. Apparently they had reached their saturation limit the day before and just needed time away from the process.

89. If the parties reach a settlement, should the parties sign an agreement before they leave the mediation session?

When the parties reach agreement, they should set forth their settlement in written form. This could be a handwritten, numbered list of the resolved issues which might include:

Payment by one party to the other.

The date the payment will be made.

The amount of interest that will accrue if not paid on the due date.

The return of goods.

The repair of goods.

Restitution of funds.

Promises not to perform certain conduct.

Promises to perform certain conduct.

Issues which were discussed and are no longer at issue (throw away items).

You can review the agreement to make sure that it contains a complete list of resolved issues. Have the parties sign the agreement that they have drafted. The parties are then free to have their attorneys add any legal language they feel necessary.

You should not sign the settlement agreement. The mediator is not a party to the agreement.

90. Who drafts the settlement agreement?

First, let me emphasize that *the mediator does not draft the settlement agreement.* The agreement which the parties have drafted may suffice, and they may not want to incur legal fees to have their attorneys draft a more detailed document. However, most parties request that their attorneys draft a settlement agreement. The parties' settlement agreement is a legal document, with legal consequences. Your function as a mediator is only to guide the parties to a settlement. You should not participate in the drafting of a legal document that binds the parties.

91. What if I believe the settlement is not fair?

It is not your responsibility to ensure the fairness of the settlement. If the parties are satisfied, and the settlement reflects their agreement as to how the dispute should end, you should not voice any dissatisfaction with the result. What may seem unfair to you may be appropriate to the parties. The extent to which parties are willing to compromise may be based upon information that was not revealed to the mediator. A desire to have the dispute settled and to get on with life may be worth more than you expect. If the parties are satisfied with the settlement, you should be also.

After the Mediation

AFTER THE MEDIATION

92. Who may decide to terminate the mediation?

Either party may decide that the mediation will not result in a settlement and ask to withdraw from the mediation. However, before the decision is made to terminate the mediation, the parties should discuss the matter with the mediator.

You can propose "a cooling off" period. Ask the parties whether they think that a recess may be more appropriate than a termination of the proceedings. You may suggest that rather than decide now to terminate the mediation, the parties confer in the next few days and inform you if they believe it would be in their interest to continue with the mediation.

93. When are my duties concluded?

Your duties are concluded when the parties reach a settlement or decide that they have exhausted all efforts to settle the matter, and there is nothing more that can be done.

94. What should I do with my notes?

Destroy them. There is no advantage or obligation to keep your notes. If a lawsuit is filed to enforce a settlement agreement, a party may attempt to subpoena your notes, even if your agreement with the parties contained a condition that they would not do so. You cannot produce notes if you have destroyed them and they no longer exist. However, as mentioned previously, if you have not destroyed your notes when you receive the subpoena, you cannot then destroy them. Destroy your notes immediately after the mediation is concluded.

95. What should I do with my copies of the parties' documents?

It is good practice to return the documents to the administering organization or to the parties directly. Often the parties do not want their documents after the mediation, but I prefer to return them to the parties.

If there is a suit to enforce the settlement, I do not want to have any documentation in my possession that would be responsive to a subpoena, nor do I wish to state that I have destroyed any documents which I had received from the parties. Your best evidence that you do not have any documents from the mediation is a copy of your transmittal letter stating you are returning all copies of documents.

96. May I discuss the outcome of the mediation?

Mediations are confidential matters between the parties. Unlike a lawsuit, they are not matters of public record. You should not, under any circumstances, reveal the identities of the parties or discuss the outcome of a mediation. This applies in perpetuity. Do not assume after several years have passed that it is safe to speak about the mediation.

97. How is a mediation settlement enforced?

The end result of a successful mediation should be a written settlement agreement signed by the parties. This is a binding contract between the parties which sets forth obligations for payment or the other mechanisms for satisfying the parties, such as return of goods, repair of damage, or other means of satisfaction. It is usually self-enforced, as the parties will abide by the agreement.

98. What if the parties do not abide by their settlement agreement?

If the terms of the settlement agreement are not fulfilled, the aggrieved party may file a lawsuit for breach of contract. Remember, once the mediation is concluded, you should have no interest in and make no inquiries about payment or enforcement of the settlement agreement.

Payment
and
Conclusion

Basic Skills for the New Mediator

PAYMENT

99. How do I arrange compensation for my services?

If you are mediating through an administering organization, the organization usually has a range of mediator's fees. The parties will agree to compensation within this range, and the case administrator will inform you as to the parties' agreement for mediator compensation.

Some organizations offer the first day of mediation at no charge for mediator's fees, as an incentive to the parties to complete the mediation quickly, and also because mediators are to a certain extent considered "volunteers" who are rendering service to the community.

Once the mediation extends more than a day, the usual arrangement is for the mediator to charge per diem or by the hour. The administering organizations will usually have the mediator sign an agreement that the parties are obligated to pay the mediator's the fee, and the administering organization is not obligated to make payment if the parties fail to do so.

For private mediations, where the parties contact the mediator directly, the mediator has more flexibility in negotiating a fee. Some mediators charge an hourly fee, while others negotiate a per diem. Some charge a per diem rate for up to eight hours of mediation time and an hourly rate for mediation sessions in excess of eight hours in a given day.

100. How do I make sure I am paid?

First, enter into a written agreement with the parties. Administering organizations will have the parties enter into an agreement to deposit the fee with them before the mediation begins, and may advise the mediator not to proceed with the mediation if the funds are not received.

If you have been retained privately, you should also have a written fee agreement directly with the parties. Have the *parties* sign the agreement, not their attorneys. I suggest that you require the parties to pay your estimated fees in advance of the mediation.

Appendix A contains a sample agreement between the mediator and the parties, which includes the agreement for compensation.

CONCLUSION

101. This is your question.

If you have a question you would like me to answer, please write, call, or e-mail.

Allan H. Goodman
SOLOMON PUBLICATIONS
P.O. Box 2124
Rockville, MD 20847-2124

phone (301)816-1025
book@solomonpublications.com
www.solomonpublications.com

I welcome suggestions or comments.

Appendices

Appendix A
Sample Agreement between the Mediator and the Parties

This agreement dated _____, 200_, between <u>Party 1</u> and <u>Party 2</u> (referred to as the "parties" and <u>Mediator</u> (referred to as the "mediator") sets forth the terms and conditions governing the mediation of the dispute between the parties arising from <u>name of project, family dispute, auto accident, etc.</u> (referred to as the "dispute").

The parties have chosen the mediator as an independent neutral to aid the parties in their attempt to settle the dispute.

The mediator will not decide who prevails in the dispute and will not render an award, verdict, or judgment, or otherwise determine fault or blame.

The parties understand that the mediator is impartial, does not favor one party over the other, and will not offer legal advice to the parties. The parties should seek legal advice from their own counsel, and counsel may attend the mediation session.

The mediation is an attempt to settle the dispute, and as such all communications before, during, and after the mediation between the parties, the mediator, and counsel are settlement discussions which are confidential and inadmissible in any subsequent litigation or arbitration.

The parties understand that there is no guarantee that the mediation will result in a settlement of the dispute. Should the mediation not result in a settlement of the dispute, and the parties proceed to litigation or arbitration or other means of dispute resolution, the parties agree that they will not subpoena or otherwise request the mediator to offer testimony or produce any documents, records, or work product.

If the parties reach a settlement of the dispute and thereafter sign a written settlement agreement, such written settlement agreement may be produced by either party in a subsequent action to enforce the settlement agreement, but the parties agree that they will not subpoena or otherwise request the mediator to offer testimony or produce any documents, records, or work product.

The mediation may be terminated at the request of either party or at the request of the mediator if the mediator determines that a resolution of the dispute will not occur as the result of the mediation.

The parties will compensate the mediator at the hourly rate of $ for the mediator's efforts, including, but not limited to, preliminary conference calls, correspondence, review of written submissions, the mediation session, and post-mediation communications. In addition, the parties will reimburse the mediator for all reasonable expenses incurred on the parties' behalf, including, but not limited to, phone charges, fax charges, travel, postage, meals, or refreshments provided during the mediation session.

The parties agree to share equally the cost of the mediation, and therefore the payment of the mediator's fees and expenses will not be an issue in the mediation. Two days before the mediation, the parties will pay the mediator $_ as payment for services rendered to date and an estimated payment for _x_ hours for the mediation session. If the mediation session is less than _x_ hours, the mediator will refund the difference to the parties. If the mediation is more than _x_ hours, the parties will pay the mediator the balance due within 5 working days of the conclusion of the mediation.

If the parties reach a settlement, the parties, and not the mediator, agree to draft a written agreement setting forth the matters decided. The parties should review this written settlement agreement with their counsel before the agreement is placed in final form.

The parties release the mediator from liability arising from any act or omission during the mediation. The parties recognize that the mediator is not counsel to any party and will not render legal services in the mediation.

Mediator

_____
Date:

Party 1:

_____
By: Date:
Position:

Party 2:

_____
By: Date:
Position:

Appendix B - Stages of Mediation

Preliminary Conference

Introduce yourself.
Briefly explain the mediation process.
Request a brief memorandum summarizing the issues and
a limited number of relevant documents.
Determine location and schedule the mediation session.

The Mediation Session

Joint Session - Fact-Finding and Issue Definition

Mediator's Opening Statement
Briefly describe your background.
State basis of empathy.
Describe the mediation process.
Praise the parties for choosing to mediate.

Parties' Opening Statements
Parties vent their emotions and frustration.
Parties state factual basis of dispute.

Ask clarification questions and list issues.

First Private Caucus - Fact-Finding and Issue Definition
Continued

Parties continue to vent emotion and frustration.
Ask the parties to rank the issues in order of importance.
Parties divulge confidential information.
Play "devil's advocate" - determine strengths and weaknesses.
Determine hidden agenda items and throw-away issues.

Second Private Caucus - Begin to Seek Resolution

Explore the parties' initial settlement offer.
Parties do not authorize transmission of settlement offer.
Determine disparity in range of initial settlement offers.

Third Private Caucus - Negotiations Begin

Request permission to make settlement offer.
Discuss possible solutions with the parties.
Brainstorm possible solutions.
Suggest possible solutions.

Fourth Private Caucus - Negotiations Continue

Parties make counteroffers - authorize you to transmit the offer.
Transmit settlement offers.
Review parties reactions to settlement offers.

Impasse in Negotiations

Recommend the parties take a break and resume the next day.
If parties believe further mediation would not be fruitful
request that they inform you within a specified period
to discontinue the mediation.
Leave door open for resuming mediation.

Continuing Private Caucuses - Leading to Final Offer

Request final offers.
Ask parties if you should transmit the offer or
if they want a joint session to discuss final offers.

Joint Session - Final Settlement

Parties meet in joint session, make final offers.

SETTLEMENT AGREED.

Closure

Have parties list points of agreement and sign the list.
Make sure there are no unsettled issues.
Thank and commend everyone.

Formal Drafting of Settlement Agreement

Settlement agreement drafted by parties or their attorneys,
not by the mediator.

Appendix C
Everything You Never Wanted to Know
About the Rules of Evidence

Do I need to know the rules of evidence?

The rules of evidence are not esoteric principles that exist solely for the benefit of lawyers and judges. We use the basic concepts of the rules of evidence every day to deal with personal and business situations.

In litigation and arbitration, judges and arbitrators apply evidentiary concepts in order to arrive at their decisions. Mediators do not "decide" the case, so they do not need to employ evidentiary concepts in the same manner as those who do make such decisions. However, you should be familiar with some basic concepts of the rules of evidence. Attorneys often use these concepts and this knowledge will help you analyze the strengths and weaknesses of a party's case.

There are three basic evidentiary concepts - **authenticity, relevancy** and **credibility**.

Authenticity deals with whether evidence such as documents or physical objects are actually what they purport to be. Was the letter actually written by the person who signed it? Was it actually written during the time period of the dispute, or is it a later fabrication? Is the soil sample actually from the construction site? You may encounter challenges to authenticity of evidence in mediation.

Relevancy concerns whether or not the evidence tends to prove or disprove a fact that is essential to a party's case. If the evidence presented does not tend to prove or disprove such a fact, there is no reason to discuss it. It is not relevant.

Credibility is the measure of how **believable** the evidence is. Lawyers sometimes refer to a credibility determination as to how much **weight** the court should accord the evidence.

We make relevancy and credibility determinations every day. When a party offers arguments to convince the other party that a fact is true, and the information does not remotely prove the point, that party is offering evidence that is not relevant.

As for credibility, you usually know when you do not believe what someone is saying. Your disbelief may come from a person's demeanor, from the way he or she speaks or acts. A person's tone of voice, hesitancy in speaking, or lack of eye contact may raise questions of credibility

You may question information because it comes from an indirect source. When you hear information secondhand or third-hand from someone who really does not have personal knowledge of what they are speaking about, you tend to question it. This is what is known as hearsay. Hearsay may actually be true, but the way it is presented to you, from someone without actual knowledge, raises questions of accuracy and reliability.

We will explore how to deal with relevancy and credibility in the context of a mediation session in more detail.

What does it mean that information is not relevant?

A comment that information is not relevant means that the information is not germane to the dispute, and therefore does not tend to prove or disprove a fact necessary to resolve the dispute. Even if you think the information is not relevant, you should allow the information to be presented to you so you can assess the relevancy yourself. In mediation, you do not run the risk of admitting improper evidence, so you should use every opportunity to gather information which might be helpful.

What is hearsay?

There are lengthy treatises written on hearsay, and a major portion of the study of evidence in law school is devoted to this topic. Hearsay is a factor in determining credibility. For our purposes, we need to define hearsay.

There is no universally accepted definition of hearsay. We can use the following definition:

***Hearsay* is a statement or assertive conduct made out of court which is offered in court to prove the truth of the matter asserted.**

Is that clear? Probably not. Generally, it means that hearsay is testimony by someone in court about something that another person said or did out of court which is offered by the witness to prove what the other individual said or did ***was true***.

That's probably still not clear. In order to illustrate this concept, we can review an example of how an objection to hearsay would be dealt with in court.

Attorney #1: What did the driver say after the accident?

Attorney #2: [Before the witness can answer]. Objection. This witness cannot testify as to what the driver said. It would be hearsay.

At this point, we still do not know why the testimony is being offered. Suppose the testimony is to prove that the driver was speeding, and the testimony is:

Witness: After the accident, I heard the driver of the car say, "I was driving too fast."

If the statement is offered to prove the *truth* of the matter asserted, i.e., the driver was driving too fast, it is what is known as an admission against interest, and admissible as evidence. Admissions against interest may or may not be considered hearsay, depending upon the rules of evidence to be applied. Under the Federal Rules of Evidence, this testimony is admissible as an admission against the interest of the party making the statement, and therefore not considered hearsay. Other rules of evidence, applied by state courts, may consider an admission against interest hearsay, but allow its admission into evidence as an exception to the hearsay rule.

What if the testimony was not being offered to prove the truth of what was said, but was being offered to prove that the driver of the car was conscious after the accident? It would then not be hearsay, as it is not offered to prove the truth of the matter asserted, i.e., that the driver was driving too fast; rather, it is offered to prove that the driver was able to and did in fact speak, and was therefore conscious.

This example shows you the dilemma one faces in dealing with testimony which is potentially hearsay. The testimony itself does not necessarily give you enough information to determine if it is hearsay. You need to know the *purpose* of the testimony.

What reaction should I have to statements that information is not relevant or hearsay?

Diplomatically inform a party that they are offering information that does not appear to be relevant, by stating, for example, "I don't quite understand how this supports your position. Perhaps you could explain the relevancy of that statement . . . ."

A party that introduces information that is not relevant into discussions should be cautioned that such information is not persuasive and reveals a weakness in the case as to the specific issue. In essence, the approach you take is "if this does not persuade me, it certainly is not going to persuade a judge or jury."

Hearsay does not necessarily reveal a weakness in the case. The party may actually be able to produce the individual that made the original statement upon which the party relies. Explore with the party the availability of the individual to offer testimony in the event the matter goes to court.

Solomon Publications offers
the companion volume
BASIC SKILLS FOR THE NEW ARBITRATOR
Available from the Publisher and your bookstore.

BASIC SKILLS FOR THE NEW ARBITRATOR provides a detailed overview of arbitration, from the prehearing phase through the hearing and deliberation of the award. It guides the new arbitrator through the arbitration process by answering the *one hundred questions most frequently* asked by new arbitrators. BASIC SKILLS FOR THE NEW ARBITRATOR has been used successfully for self-instruction and as a training text. It is not just for new arbitrators! Experienced arbitrators and attorneys involved in arbitration will find this book extremely useful. The discussion of evidentiary concepts is especially valuable for arbitrators who must deal with the vocabulary of the legal profession.

You will learn to:

Provide necessary ethical disclosures
Conduct a preliminary conference
Issue prehearing orders
Establish a discovery schedule
Resolve discovery disputes
Deal with attempts to delay the hearing
Preside at a hearing
Avoid prejudicial conduct

SOLOMON PUBLICATIONS PO Box 2124 Rockville, Maryland 20847
phone (301) 816-1025
book@solomonpublications.com
www.solomonpublications.com